SLEEP APNEA EDUCATION FOR HEALTHCARE PROVIDERS

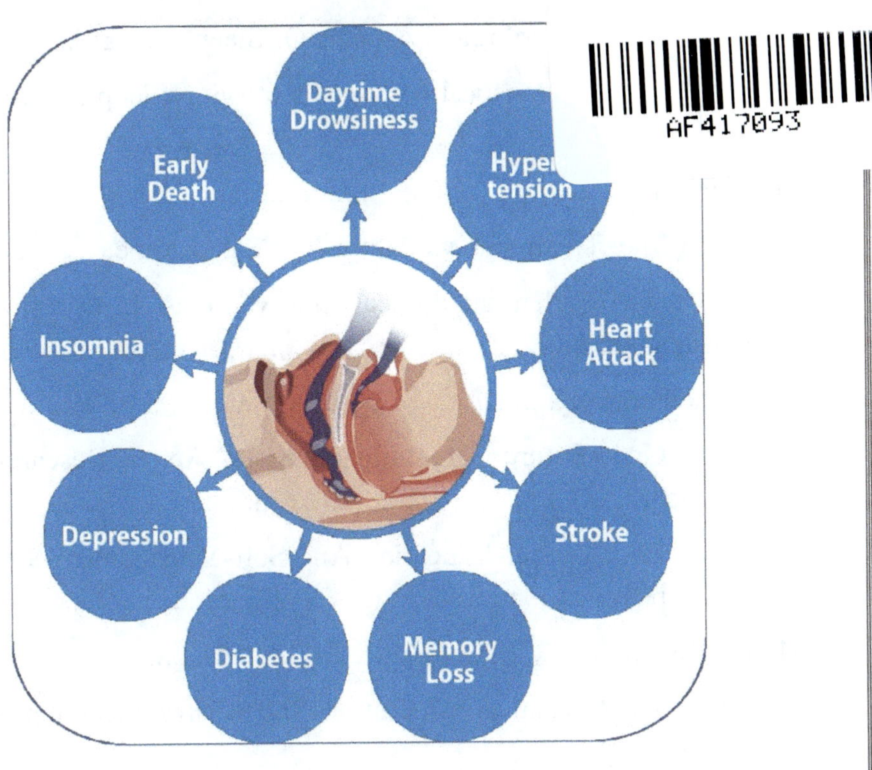

TABLE OF CONTENTS

COURSE OVERVIEW:

This comprehensive course on Sleep Apnea Education for Healthcare Providers is designed to equip respiratory therapists, doctors, nurses, and other healthcare professionals with an in-depth understanding of sleep apnea. The course covers the full spectrum of knowledge required to diagnose, treat, and manage sleep apnea in diverse patient populations. Participants will learn about the clinical and physiological signs of sleep apnea, diagnostic tools and techniques, various treatment options including CPAP and medications, as well as the impact of lifestyle interventions.

COURSE OBJECTIVES:

By the end of this course, participants will be able to: Understand the Pathophysiology of Sleep Apnea; Identify Clinical Signs and Symptoms; Utilize Diagnostic Tools and Techniques; Develop Effective Treatment Plans; Manage Special Populations; Implement Patient Education and Self-Management Strategies; Integrate Telemedicine in Sleep Apnea Care; Engage in Multidisciplinary Collaboration This course aims to provide healthcare providers with the knowledge and tools necessary to deliver comprehensive, informed, and compassionate care to patients with sleep apnea. Through enhanced understanding and application of the latest practices and technologies, participants will be well-equipped to address the complex needs of this patient population

COURSE MATERIALS

To learn this course, **healthcare providers/ participants** must be provided with materials like a Pen, pencil, notebook, and notepad to better understand and make it easy for them to learn.

INTRODUCTION

Sleep apnea is a pervasive and often underdiagnosed condition that significantly impacts patients' health and quality of life. For healthcare providers, understanding sleep apnea in depth is crucial for providing comprehensive care and improving patient outcomes. This book, "Mastering Sleep Apnea: A Comprehensive Guide for Healthcare Providers," aims to equip respiratory therapists, doctors, and nurses with the knowledge and skills necessary to effectively diagnose, treat, and manage sleep apnea.

Sleep apnea is characterized by repeated interruptions in breathing during sleep, leading to reduced oxygen levels and fragmented sleep. These interruptions, or apneas, can be obstructive, central, or mixed. Obstructive sleep apnea (OSA) is the most common form, where the airway becomes blocked, often by soft tissue in the throat. Central sleep apnea (CSA) occurs when the brain fails to send appropriate signals to the muscles that control breathing. Mixed sleep apnea is a combination of both.

The importance of addressing sleep apnea cannot be overstated. Untreated sleep apnea is associated with numerous health complications, including hypertension, cardiovascular disease, stroke, diabetes, and impaired cognitive function. Moreover, it affects daily functioning, leading to excessive daytime sleepiness, decreased alertness, and an increased risk of motor vehicle this book aims to improve patient outcomes by empowering healthcare providers with the tools and information needed to address sleep apnea comprehensively.

MODULE ONE

LESSON ONE: UNDERSTANDING SLEEP APNEA

Sleep apnea is a sleep disorder characterized by repeated interruptions in breathing during sleep. These interruptions, or apneas, can last from a few seconds to minutes and may occur multiple times per hour. The three main types of sleep apnea are obstructive sleep apnea (OSA), central sleep apnea (CSA), and mixed sleep apnea, each with distinct pathophysiological mechanisms and clinical implications.

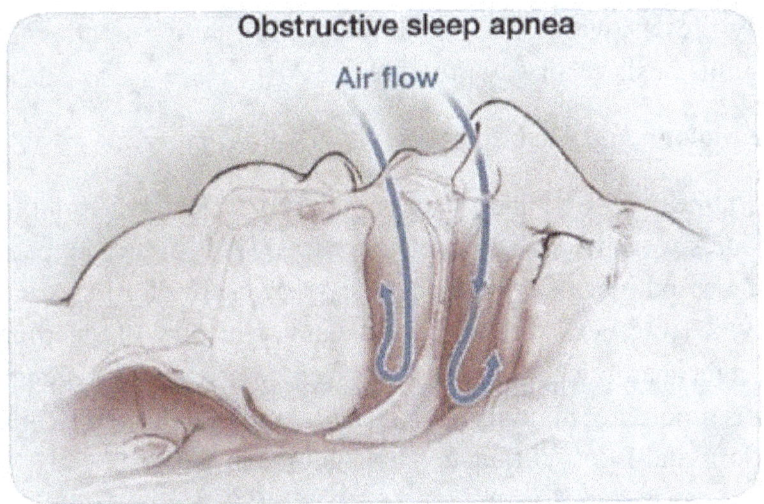

TYPES OF SLEEP APNEA

1. Obstructive Sleep Apnea (OSA)

OSA is the most prevalent form of sleep apnea. It occurs when the muscles in the throat relax excessively during sleep, leading to a partial or complete blockage of the airway. This obstruction prevents air from flowing into the lungs, despite the body's efforts to breathe. Common causes of airway obstruction include enlarged tonsils, a large tongue, obesity, and structural abnormalities in the airway.

2. Central Sleep Apnea (CSA)

CSA is less common and occurs when the brain fails to send appropriate signals to the muscles that control breathing. Unlike OSA, there is no physical blockage of the airway. Instead, the problem lies in the central nervous system's regulation of breathing. CSA is often associated with underlying medical conditions such as heart failure, stroke, and other neurological disorders.

3. Mixed Sleep Apnea

Mixed sleep apnea, also known as complex sleep apnea syndrome, is a combination of OSA and CSA. Patients with mixed sleep apnea initially present with OSA but develop CSA during treatment with continuous positive airway pressure (CPAP).

Epidemiology and Risk Factors

Sleep apnea is a widespread condition affecting millions of individuals worldwide. The prevalence of OSA is higher in men than in women and increases with age. Key risk factors for OSA include obesity, a large neck circumference, family history of sleep apnea, and certain anatomical features such as a recessed jaw or large tonsils. CSA is more commonly associated with underlying medical conditions and is less influenced by anatomical factors.

Pathophysiology of Sleep Apnea

The pathophysiology of sleep apnea involves complex interactions between anatomical, neuromuscular, and physiological factors. In OSA, the airway collapse is primarily due to the relaxation of the pharyngeal muscles during sleep, which reduces the patency of the upper airway. This collapse leads to repeated episodes of hypoxia (low oxygen levels) and hypercapnia (high carbon dioxide levels), triggering arousals from sleep to reopen the airway.

In CSA, the underlying issue is the instability of the respiratory control centers in the brain. This instability can be caused by conditions such as heart failure, which affects the feedback mechanisms involved in respiratory control. The result is a periodic cessation of breathing, leading to fluctuations in blood oxygen levels.

Symptoms and Clinical Presentation

The symptoms of sleep apnea can vary widely among individuals. Common symptoms include:

- Loud snoring
- Episodes of breathing cessation witnessed by a bed partner
- Excessive daytime sleepiness
- Morning headaches
- Difficulty concentrating
- Irritability and mood changes
- Insomnia or difficulty staying asleep

In addition to these symptoms, patients with OSA may experience nocturia (frequent nighttime urination), gastroesophageal reflux disease (GERD), and decreased libido. CSA symptoms often overlap with those of OSA but may also include symptoms related to the underlying medical condition.

Complications of Untreated Sleep Apnea

Untreated sleep apnea can lead to numerous health complications. Chronic intermittent hypoxia and sleep fragmentation contribute to the development of cardiovascular diseases, including hypertension, heart failure, and arrhythmias. There is also an increased risk of stroke, metabolic disorders such as diabetes, and neurocognitive impairment. The daytime sleepiness associated with sleep apnea can significantly impair daily functioning, increasing the risk of motor vehicle accidents and occupational injuries.

Diagnosis of Sleep Apnea

The diagnosis of sleep apnea typically involves a thorough clinical evaluation, including a detailed medical history and physical examination. The gold standard for diagnosing sleep apnea is polysomnography (PSG), an overnight sleep study conducted in a sleep laboratory. PSG records various physiological parameters, including brain activity, eye movements, muscle activity, heart rate, and respiratory effort.

Home sleep apnea testing (HSAT) is an alternative diagnostic method for patients with a high pretest probability of moderate to severe OSA. HSAT involves the use of portable monitoring devices that record respiratory parameters during sleep at home.

Understanding sleep apnea is the first step in providing effective care for patients with this condition. By recognizing the types, risk factors, pathophysiology, symptoms, and complications of sleep apnea, healthcare providers can better identify and manage this disorder. In the subsequent lesson, we will explore the clinical signs, diagnostic imaging, and treatment modalities in greater detail, equipping you with the knowledge and skills to address sleep apnea comprehensively

DISCUSSION QUESTIONS

- What are the primary physiological mechanisms that lead to obstructive sleep apnea, and how do these mechanisms differ from those causing central sleep apnea?
- How can healthcare providers effectively educate patients about the different types of sleep apnea and their associated risks and symptoms?

LESSON TWO: CLINICAL SIGNS AND SYMPTOMS OF SLEEP APNEA

The clinical presentation of sleep apnea can vary significantly among patients, making it essential for healthcare providers to be adept at recognizing its diverse manifestations. Sleep apnea often presents with a range of symptoms that can affect various aspects of a patient's life. Understanding these clinical signs and symptoms is crucial for early detection and effective management.

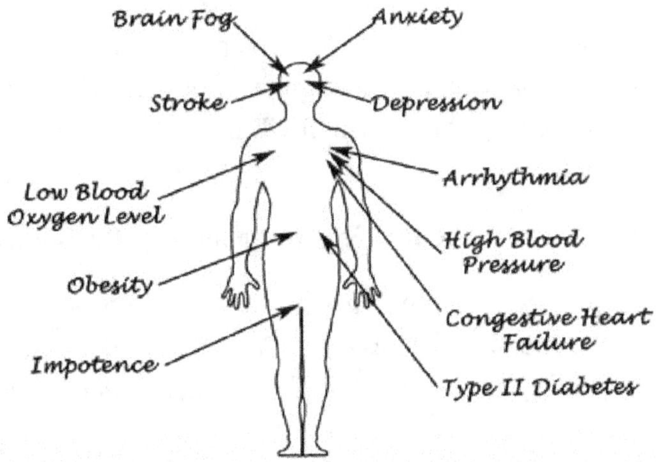

Common Clinical Signs

1. Loud Snoring

One of the hallmark signs of obstructive sleep apnea (OSA) is loud and chronic snoring. This occurs due to the partial blockage of the airway, causing vibrations in the throat tissues as air passes through. While not all individuals who snore have OSA, persistent and loud snoring is a significant indicator.

2. Witnessed Apneas

Bed partners often report episodes where the patient stops breathing during sleep. These apneas are typically followed by choking or gasping sounds as the patient resumes breathing. Witnessed apneas are a critical clue in the diagnosis of sleep apnea.

3. Excessive Daytime Sleepiness (EDS)

Patients with sleep apnea frequently experience excessive daytime sleepiness, even after a full night's sleep. EDS can lead to difficulties staying awake during daytime activities, decreased productivity, and an increased risk of accidents.

4. Morning Headaches

Morning headaches are common in sleep apnea patients, likely due to the nocturnal hypoxia and hypercapnia experienced during apneic episodes. These headaches are usually dull and located at the front or sides of the head.

5. Difficulty Concentrating and Memory Problems

Cognitive impairment, including difficulty concentrating, memory problems, and reduced alertness, is often reported by sleep apnea patients. These issues stem from fragmented sleep and reduced oxygen supply to the brain.

Less Common Clinical Signs

1. Nocturia

Frequent nighttime urination, known as nocturia, is commonly seen in patients with OSA. The exact mechanism is not entirely understood, but it is believed to be related to the increased production of atrial natriuretic peptide (ANP) during apneic events.

2. Dry Mouth and Sore Throat

Many sleep apnea patients wake up with a dry mouth or sore throat. This can result from mouth breathing during sleep due to partial airway obstruction.

3. Mood Changes and Irritability

Chronic sleep disruption can lead to significant mood changes, including irritability, depression, and anxiety. These mood disturbances further impact the patient's quality of life and overall well-being.

4. Gastroesophageal Reflux Disease (GERD)

There is a strong association between sleep apnea and GERD. The increased intra-thoracic pressure during apneas can lead to the reflux of stomach contents into the esophagus, causing GERD symptoms.

CLINICAL EVALUATION AND HISTORY TAKING

1. Detailed Sleep History

A comprehensive sleep history is essential for identifying sleep apnea. Questions should address the duration and quality of sleep, the presence of snoring, witnessed apneas, and the patient's sleep habits.

2. Assessment of Daytime Symptoms

Evaluating daytime symptoms such as excessive sleepiness, fatigue, and cognitive impairment helps to gauge the impact of sleep apnea on daily functioning. The Epworth Sleepiness Scale (ESS) is a valuable tool for quantifying daytime sleepiness.

3. Medical and Family History

A thorough medical history should include questions about comorbid conditions such as hypertension, heart disease, diabetes, and stroke.

A family history of sleep apnea or related disorders can also provide important diagnostic clues.

Physical Examination

1. **Body Mass Index (BMI):** Obesity is a significant risk factor for OSA. Calculating the BMI helps to assess the degree of obesity and its potential contribution to airway obstruction.
2. **Neck Circumference:** An increased neck circumference is associated with a higher risk of OSA. A neck circumference greater than 17 inches in men and 16 inches in women is considered a risk factor.
3. **Airway Examination:** Examining the airway for anatomical abnormalities such as enlarged tonsils, a large tongue, or a recessed jaw can help identify potential causes of airway obstruction.
4. **Blood Pressure Measurement:** Hypertension is commonly seen in sleep apnea patients. Monitoring blood pressure is important for identifying and managing this comorbidity.

Recognizing the clinical signs and symptoms of sleep apnea is crucial for early diagnosis and intervention. Healthcare providers must be vigilant in identifying these signs during patient evaluations. By understanding the diverse manifestations of sleep apnea and conducting thorough clinical assessments, providers can ensure timely and effective management, improving patient outcomes and quality of life.

DISCUSSION QUESTIONS

- What are the most common clinical signs and symptoms of sleep apnea that healthcare providers should be aware of during patient evaluations?
- How can the presence of comorbid conditions, such as obesity or cardiovascular disease, influence the presentation and diagnosis of sleep apnea?

MODULE TWO

LESSON ONE: PHYSIOLOGICAL ASPECTS OF SLEEP APNEA

The physiological aspects of sleep apnea involve complex interactions between anatomical, neuromuscular, and biochemical factors. Understanding these underlying mechanisms is crucial for healthcare providers to diagnose and manage sleep apnea effectively. This lesson delves into the physiological processes that contribute to the development and progression of sleep apnea.

Anatomy and Physiology of the Upper Airway

1. Anatomical Considerations

The upper airway, which includes the nasal passages, pharynx, and larynx, plays a critical role in maintaining airway patency during sleep. In individuals with obstructive sleep apnea (OSA), anatomical factors such as a narrow airway, enlarged tonsils, or a large tongue can predispose them to airway collapse.

2. Neuromuscular Control

During wakefulness, the upper airway muscles maintain tone and keep the airway open. However, during sleep, especially during rapid eye movement (REM) sleep, there is a natural reduction in muscle tone. In OSA patients, this reduction is exaggerated, leading to airway collapse and obstruction.

3. The Role of the Soft Palate and Tongue

The soft palate and tongue are key structures in the upper airway. In OSA, the soft palate may relax and fall backward, obstructing the airway. Similarly, the tongue can fall back against the pharyngeal wall, further contributing to airway obstruction.

RESPIRATORY CONTROL AND CENTRAL SLEEP APNEA

1. Central Respiratory Centers

Central sleep apnea (CSA) is characterized by a failure of the brain to send appropriate signals to the respiratory muscles. The central respiratory centers, located in the brainstem, regulate breathing by responding to changes in blood levels of oxygen and carbon dioxide.

2. Chemoreceptor Sensitivity

Chemoreceptors in the carotid bodies and aortic arch detect changes in blood gases and relay this information to the brainstem. In CSA, there may be an abnormal response to these signals, leading to periods of apnea.

3. Heart Failure and CSA

Heart failure is a common cause of CSA. In heart failure patients, fluid accumulation in the lungs and altered blood flow can disrupt the normal feedback mechanisms involved in respiratory control, resulting in periodic breathing and apneas.

Pathophysiological Mechanisms of Sleep Apnea

1. Intermittent Hypoxia

Repeated episodes of airway obstruction in OSA lead to intermittent hypoxia, where blood oxygen levels drop during apneas and rise upon arousal. Intermittent hypoxia is associated with oxidative stress, inflammation, and endothelial dysfunction, contributing to cardiovascular complications.

2. Sleep Fragmentation

Frequent arousals during sleep result in fragmented sleep architecture. This sleep fragmentation impairs the restorative functions of sleep, leading to excessive daytime sleepiness, cognitive impairment, and mood disturbances.

3. Sympathetic Nervous System Activation

Both OSA and CSA are associated with increased sympathetic nervous system activity. Intermittent hypoxia and arousals trigger the release of stress hormones such as adrenaline, leading to elevated heart rate, blood pressure, and vascular resistance.

4. Metabolic Dysregulation

Sleep apnea is linked to metabolic disturbances, including insulin resistance and dyslipidemia. The chronic intermittent hypoxia and sleep fragmentation associated with sleep apnea can disrupt glucose metabolism and promote the development of type 2 diabetes and metabolic syndrome.

Cardiovascular Implications

1. Hypertension

The repeated episodes of hypoxia and sympathetic activation in sleep apnea contribute to the development of hypertension. Both daytime and nocturnal blood pressure can be elevated in sleep apnea patients.

2. Heart Failure and Arrhythmias

Sleep apnea increases the risk of developing heart failure and cardiac arrhythmias. The negative intrathoracic pressure generated during apneas can place a strain on the heart, while intermittent hypoxia can lead to structural and electrical remodeling of the heart.

3. Stroke and Cerebrovascular Disease

There is a strong association between sleep apnea and stroke. The combination of hypertension, increased sympathetic activity, and endothelial dysfunction in sleep apnea patients increases the risk of cerebrovascular events.

The physiological aspects of sleep apnea involve intricate interactions between anatomical structures, neuromuscular control, and biochemical processes. Understanding these mechanisms is essential for healthcare providers to effectively diagnose and manage sleep apnea. By recognizing the pathophysiological processes underlying sleep apnea, providers can better appreciate the condition's impact on overall health and develop comprehensive treatment plans to improve patient outcomes.

DISCUSSION QUESTIONS

- How do polysomnography and home sleep apnea testing compare in terms of accuracy, patient convenience, and overall effectiveness for diagnosing sleep apnea?

- What are the potential limitations of using diagnostic imaging, such as X-rays or MRIs, for identifying sleep apnea, and how can these limitations be addressed?

LESSON TWO: DIAGNOSTIC IMAGING: IDENTIFYING SLEEP APNEA ON X-RAYS

Diagnostic imaging plays a crucial role in the evaluation of sleep apnea. While polysomnography remains the gold standard for diagnosing sleep apnea, imaging studies such as X-rays can provide valuable insights into the anatomical factors contributing to airway obstruction. This lesson focuses on the role of X-rays in identifying sleep apnea and understanding its anatomical underpinnings.

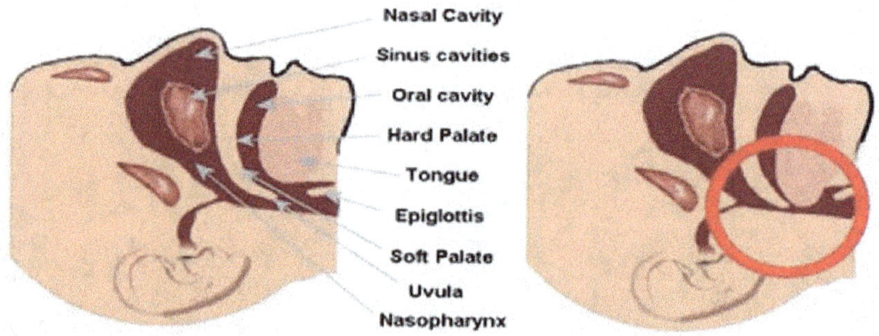

The Role of Imaging in Sleep Apnea Diagnosis

Polysomnography vs. Imaging

Polysomnography (PSG) is the definitive diagnostic tool for sleep apnea, providing comprehensive data on sleep architecture, respiratory events, and oxygen saturation. However, imaging studies, including X-rays, CT scans, and MRIs, offer additional information about the anatomical features of the airway that may predispose patients to sleep apnea.

Importance of Anatomical Assessment

Anatomical abnormalities are significant contributors to obstructive sleep apnea (OSA). Identifying these abnormalities through imaging can guide treatment decisions, such as surgical interventions or the use of oral appliances.

Types of X-rays Used in Sleep Apnea Evaluation

1. Lateral Cephalometric Radiographs

Lateral cephalometric radiographs are commonly used in the assessment of OSA. These X-rays provide a lateral view of the head and neck, allowing for the evaluation of skeletal and soft tissue structures. Key measurements obtained from these radiographs include the size and position of the tongue, soft palate, and the dimensions of the upper airway.

2. Panoramic X-rays

Panoramic X-rays offer a broad view of the jaw and dental structures. While not as detailed as cephalometric radiographs, panoramic X-rays can help identify dental and skeletal anomalies that may contribute to airway obstruction.

Anatomical Features Assessed on X-rays

1. Airway Diameter

The diameter of the upper airway is a critical parameter in the assessment of OSA. Narrowing of the airway, particularly at the level of the oropharynx or hypopharynx, is a common finding in OSA patients. Lateral cephalometric radiographs can measure the minimum airway diameter and identify areas of narrowing.

2. Soft Palate and Uvula

The length and position of the soft palate and uvula are important factors in airway patency. A long or thick soft palate can obstruct the airway, particularly during sleep when muscle tone decreases. X-rays can help measure the soft palate length and identify any abnormalities.

3. Tongue Size and Position

An enlarged tongue, or macroglossia, is a significant risk factor for OSA. Lateral cephalometric radiographs can assess the size and position of the tongue relative to the airway. A posteriorly positioned tongue can contribute to airway obstruction.

4. Mandibular and Maxillary Structures

The skeletal structure of the mandible and maxilla can influence airway patency. A recessed jaw (retrognathia) or a narrow maxilla can reduce the size of the upper airway. Imaging studies can help assess these skeletal features and their impact on airway dimensions.

5. Hyoid Bone Position

The position of the hyoid bone is another important anatomical consideration. A low hyoid bone position is often associated with OSA. Cephalometric radiographs can measure the vertical distance between the hyoid bone and the mandibular plane, providing insight into its contribution to airway obstruction.

Clinical Implications of Imaging Findings

1. Guiding Treatment Decisions

The anatomical information obtained from X-rays can guide treatment decisions for OSA patients. For example, significant skeletal abnormalities may indicate the need for surgical interventions such as maxillomandibular advancement (MMA) or uvulopalatopharyngoplasty (UPPP).

2. Monitoring Treatment Outcomes

Imaging studies can also be used to monitor the outcomes of surgical or non-surgical treatments. Post-treatment X-rays can assess changes in airway dimensions and the position of anatomical structures, helping to evaluate the effectiveness of interventions.

3. Identifying Comorbid Conditions

In addition to assessing anatomical features related to sleep apnea, imaging studies can help identify comorbid conditions that may impact treatment and management. For instance, sinus abnormalities or temporomandibular joint (TMJ) disorders may be detected on panoramic X-rays.

X-rays and other imaging studies are valuable tools in the evaluation of sleep apnea. They provide critical information about the anatomical features that contribute to airway obstruction, guiding treatment decisions and monitoring outcomes. By understanding the role of diagnostic imaging in sleep apnea, healthcare providers can enhance their diagnostic capabilities and improve the management of this condition.

DISCUSSION QUESTIONS

- How does sleep apnea affect cardiovascular health, and what mechanisms underlie the increased risk of hypertension and heart disease in these patients?
- What are the long-term cognitive and mental health implications of untreated sleep apnea, and how can early intervention help mitigate these effects?

MODULE THREE

LESSON ONE: TREATMENT MODALITIES FOR SLEEP APNEA

The management of sleep apnea involves a range of treatment modalities aimed at reducing apneic events, improving sleep quality, and mitigating associated health risks. This lesson explores the various treatment options for sleep apnea, including lifestyle modifications, non-pharmacological therapies, and surgical interventions.

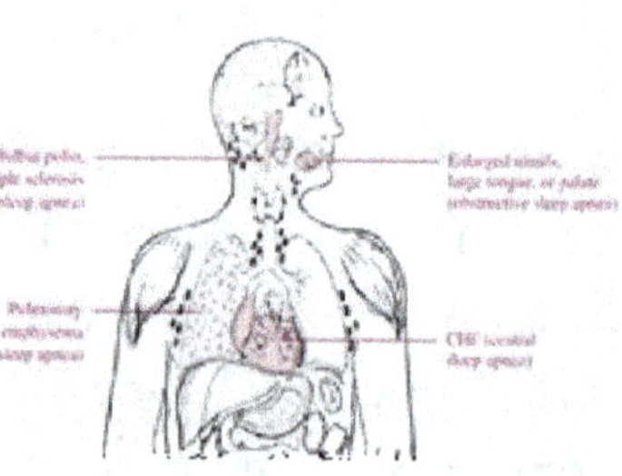

Lifestyle Modifications

1. **Weight Management**
   - Obesity is a significant risk factor for obstructive sleep apnea (OSA). Weight loss can reduce the severity of OSA by decreasing fat deposits around the upper airway, improving

airway patency. Lifestyle interventions, including diet and exercise, are crucial for weight management in OSA patients.

2. **Positional Therapy**
   - Positional therapy involves strategies to prevent patients from sleeping on their backs, where apneas are often more frequent and severe. Devices such as positional pillows or vibrating alarms can encourage side-sleeping, reducing the occurrence of apneas.

3. **Avoidance of Alcohol and Sedatives**
   - Alcohol and sedatives can relax the muscles of the upper airway, exacerbating airway obstruction. Patients with sleep apnea are advised to avoid these substances, particularly before bedtime.

4. **Smoking Cessation**
   - Smoking can cause inflammation and edema of the upper airway, worsening OSA symptoms. Smoking cessation is an important lifestyle modification for improving overall respiratory health and reducing sleep apnea severity.

Non-Pharmacological Therapies

1. **Continuous Positive Airway Pressure (CPAP)**
   - CPAP is the most effective non-pharmacological treatment for OSA. It involves the use of a machine that delivers a continuous stream of air through a mask, keeping the airway open during sleep. CPAP improves oxygenation, reduces apneic events, and alleviates daytime sleepiness.

2. **Bilevel Positive Airway Pressure (BiPAP)**
   - BiPAP provides two levels of pressure: a higher pressure during inhalation and a lower pressure during exhalation. It is often used for patients who cannot tolerate CPAP or have central sleep apnea (CSA).

3. **Oral Appliance**
   - Oral appliances, such as mandibular advancement devices (MADs), are used to treat mild to moderate OSA. These

devices reposition the lower jaw and tongue to keep the airway open during sleep. They are an alternative for patients who cannot tolerate CPAP.

4. **Behavioral Therapies**
   - Cognitive-behavioral therapy (CBT) for insomnia (CBT-I) can be beneficial for patients with comorbid insomnia and sleep apnea. Behavioral therapies can help improve sleep hygiene and address maladaptive sleep behaviors.

Surgical Interventions

1. **Uvulopalatopharyngoplasty (UPPP)**
   - UPPP is a surgical procedure that involves removing excess tissue from the soft palate, uvula, and pharynx to widen the airway. It is typically considered for patients with moderate to severe OSA who do not respond to CPAP or oral appliances.

2. **Maxillomandibular Advancement (MMA)**
   - MMA is a more extensive surgical procedure that involves repositioning the upper and lower jaws to enlarge the airway. It is effective for patients with severe OSA and significant craniofacial abnormalities.

3. **Genioglossus Advancement (GA)**
   - GA involves repositioning the genioglossus muscle (a muscle of the tongue) to prevent airway collapse. This procedure is often combined with other surgical interventions for better outcomes.

4. **Hypoglossal Nerve Stimulation**
   - Hypoglossal nerve stimulation is a newer surgical treatment for OSA. It involves implanting a device that stimulates the hypoglossal nerve, which controls tongue movements, to maintain airway patency during sleep.

Alternative and Adjunctive Therapies

1. **Orofacial Myofunctional Therapy (OMT)**
   - OMT involves exercises to strengthen the muscles of the tongue, mouth, and throat. It can be an effective adjunctive therapy for improving airway function and reducing the severity of OSA.
2. **Weight Loss Surgery**
   - Bariatric surgery may be considered for patients with severe obesity and OSA. Weight loss surgery can lead to significant improvements in OSA symptoms and overall health.
3. **Pharmacotherapy**
   - While pharmacotherapy is not typically the primary treatment for OSA, certain medications may be used to address comorbid conditions or symptoms. For example, medications for nasal congestion or GERD can help improve breathing during sleep.

The treatment of sleep apnea involves a multidisciplinary approach, incorporating lifestyle modifications, non-pharmacological therapies, and surgical interventions. By understanding the various treatment modalities available, healthcare providers can develop individualized treatment plans that address the unique needs of each patient, ultimately improving outcomes and enhancing quality of life.

DISCUSSION QUESTIONS

- What are the key factors that influence patient adherence to CPAP therapy, and what strategies can healthcare providers use to improve adherence rates?
- How do alternative treatments, such as oral appliances or surgical interventions, compare to CPAP therapy in terms of effectiveness and patient outcomes?

LESSON TWO: PHARMACOLOGICAL INTERVENTIONS IN SLEEP APNEA MANAGEMENT

Pharmacological interventions in sleep apnea management are generally adjunctive to primary treatments such as CPAP and lifestyle modifications. This lesson explores the role of medications in managing sleep apnea and its associated symptoms, including pharmacotherapy for comorbid conditions.

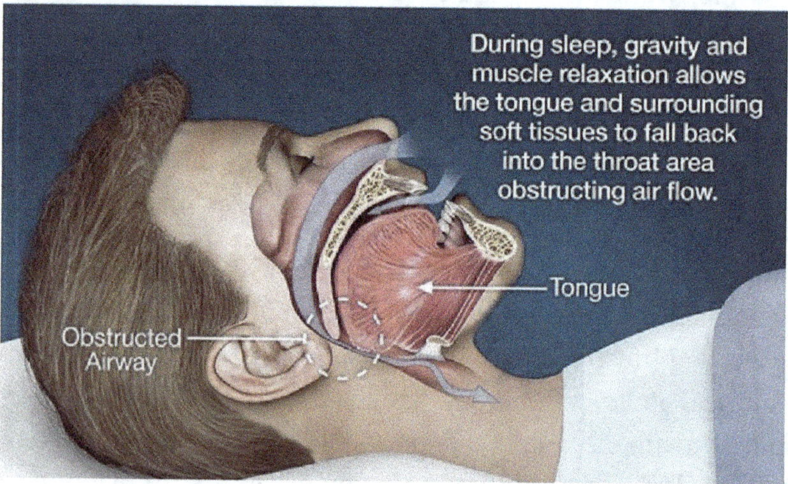

Medications for Sleep Apnea

1. **Stimulants for Excessive Daytime Sleepiness (EDS)**
   - Modafinil and armodafinil are wakefulness-promoting agents used to treat EDS in patients with obstructive sleep apnea (OSA). These medications help improve alertness and reduce the impact of daytime sleepiness on daily functioning. However, they do not address the underlying airway obstruction and should be used in conjunction with primary treatments.

2. **Antidepressants**
   - Certain antidepressants, such as selective serotonin reuptake inhibitors (SSRIs) and tricyclic antidepressants (TCAs), can have a positive effect on sleep apnea by increasing upper airway muscle tone. However, their use is limited due to side effects and variable efficacy.
3. **Acetazolamide**
   - Acetazolamide is a carbonic anhydrase inhibitor used primarily for central sleep apnea (CSA). It helps to stabilize breathing patterns by reducing the sensitivity of the brain's respiratory centers to changes in blood carbon dioxide levels.
4. **Oxygen Therapy**
   - Supplemental oxygen may be used in patients with CSA or severe OSA who experience significant oxygen desaturation during sleep. Oxygen therapy can help maintain adequate blood oxygen levels and reduce the frequency of apneic events.

Medications for Heart Failure

- Heart failure is a frequent comorbidity in CSA patients. Medications such as beta-blockers, ACE inhibitors, and diuretics are essential for managing heart failure symptoms and improving overall cardiac function.

Medications for Diabetes

- Sleep apnea is associated with insulin resistance and type 2 diabetes. Managing blood glucose levels with medications such as metformin, insulin, or other antidiabetic agents is crucial for patients with comorbid diabetes.

GERD Medications

- Gastroesophageal reflux disease (GERD) is common in sleep apnea patients. Proton pump inhibitors (PPIs) and H2-receptor antagonists can help manage GERD symptoms and improve sleep quality by reducing nighttime reflux.

Investigational Pharmacological Treatments

1. **Cannabinoids**
   - Research on cannabinoids for sleep apnea treatment is ongoing. Some studies suggest that certain cannabinoids may improve respiratory stability during sleep. However, more research is needed to establish their safety and efficacy.
2. **Serotonin Modulators**
   - Serotonin plays a role in regulating upper airway muscle tone. Investigational drugs that modulate serotonin receptors are being studied for their potential to treat OSA by enhancing airway patency.

While pharmacological interventions are not the primary treatment for sleep apnea, they play a valuable role in managing associated symptoms and comorbid conditions. Understanding the appropriate use of medications in sleep apnea management allows healthcare providers to offer comprehensive care and improve patient outcomes. Ongoing research continues to explore new pharmacological approaches to enhance the treatment of sleep apnea.

DISCUSSION QUESTIONS

- What role do medications play in the management of sleep apnea, and what are the potential benefits and risks associated with pharmacological treatment?
- How can healthcare providers determine when medication is an appropriate adjunct to other sleep apnea treatments, such as CPAP or lifestyle modifications?

MODULE FOUR

LESSON ONE: FUTURE DIRECTIONS IN SLEEP APNEA RESEARCH AND TREATMENT

The field of sleep apnea research and treatment is continually evolving. Advances in technology, new treatment modalities, and ongoing research efforts hold promise for improving the diagnosis and management of sleep apnea. This lesson explores emerging trends and future directions in sleep apnea research and treatment.

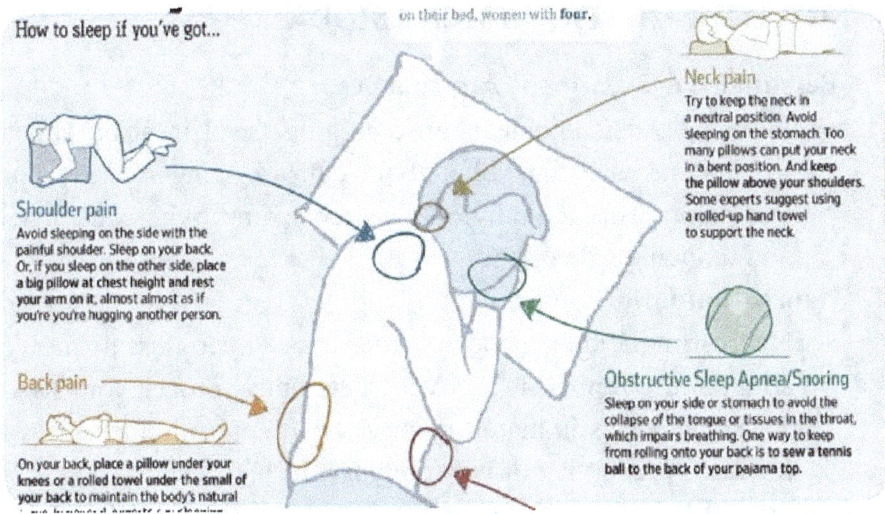

Advances in Diagnostic Technology

1. **Home Sleep Testing**
   - Home sleep apnea testing (HSAT) is becoming increasingly popular as an alternative to in-lab polysomnography. Advances in portable monitoring devices and telemedicine have made it easier for patients to undergo sleep studies in the comfort of their own homes.

2. **Wearable Devices**
   - Wearable devices that monitor sleep patterns, respiratory events, and oxygen saturation are gaining traction. These devices offer continuous monitoring and can provide valuable data for diagnosing and managing sleep apnea.
3. **Artificial Intelligence (AI) and Machine Learning**
   - AI and machine learning algorithms are being developed to analyze sleep study data more efficiently. These technologies can help identify patterns and predict treatment outcomes, enhancing the accuracy and efficiency of sleep apnea diagnosis.

INNOVATIONS IN TREATMENT MODALITIES

1. **Personalized Treatment Approaches**
   - Personalized medicine is an emerging trend in sleep apnea treatment. Genetic and phenotypic data are being used to tailor treatment plans to individual patients, improving outcomes and reducing side effects.
2. **Neurostimulation Devices**
   - Neurostimulation devices, such as hypoglossal nerve stimulators, represent a novel treatment approach for OSA. These devices stimulate the nerves that control upper airway muscles, preventing airway collapse during sleep.
3. **Advanced CPAP Technologies**
   - Continuous positive airway pressure (CPAP) technology is continually evolving. New CPAP machines offer advanced features such as auto-adjusting pressure settings, integrated humidifiers, and improved mask designs to enhance comfort and adherence.
4. **Minimally Invasive Surgical Techniques**
   - Advances in minimally invasive surgical techniques are improving the safety and efficacy of surgical treatments for OSA. Techniques such as radiofrequency ablation and laser-

assisted uvulopalatoplasty (LAUP) offer less invasive options for airway remodeling.

Research on Comorbid Conditions

1. **Cardiovascular Research**
   - Ongoing research is exploring the complex relationship between sleep apnea and cardiovascular disease. Understanding the mechanisms linking these conditions can lead to better treatment strategies and improved cardiovascular outcomes.

2. **Metabolic Health**
   - Research on the impact of sleep apnea on metabolic health is shedding light on the bidirectional relationship between sleep apnea and conditions such as obesity and diabetes. This research may lead to integrated treatment approaches that address both sleep apnea and metabolic disorders.

3. **Neurocognitive Effects**
   - Studies on the neurocognitive effects of sleep apnea are revealing the impact of sleep disruption on brain function and mental health. Understanding these effects can inform interventions to mitigate cognitive decline and mood disturbances in sleep apnea patients.

Future Directions in Public Health and Policy

1. **Awareness and Education**
   - Increasing public awareness and education about sleep apnea is crucial for early diagnosis and treatment. Public health campaigns and educational programs can help identify at-risk populations and encourage them to seek evaluation and treatment.

2. **Access to Care**
   - Ensuring access to sleep apnea diagnosis and treatment is a key public health goal. Efforts to expand healthcare coverage

and reduce barriers to care can improve outcomes for individuals with sleep apnea.

3. **Research Funding and Collaboration**
   - Continued funding for sleep apnea research is essential for advancing our understanding and treatment of the condition. Collaborative efforts among researchers, healthcare providers, and policymakers can drive innovation and improve patient care.

The future of sleep apnea research and treatment is promising, with advances in technology, personalized medicine, and a growing understanding of the condition's impact on overall health. By embracing these emerging trends and continuing to invest in research and innovation, the healthcare community can improve the diagnosis, management, and outcomes of sleep apnea for patients worldwide.

DISCUSSION QUESTIONS

- How can weight loss and physical activity specifically impact the severity of sleep apnea, and what evidence supports these lifestyle interventions?
- What are the challenges of implementing behavioral therapy for sleep apnea, and how can healthcare providers support patients in making sustainable lifestyle changes?

LESSON TWO: PATIENT EDUCATION AND SELF-MANAGEMENT STRATEGIES FOR SLEEP APNEA

Effective management of sleep apnea extends beyond clinical interventions to include patient education and self-management strategies. Educating patients about their condition and empowering them with self-management skills can significantly improve treatment adherence and outcomes. This lesson provides an overview of patient education principles, practical self-management strategies, and resources for ongoing support.

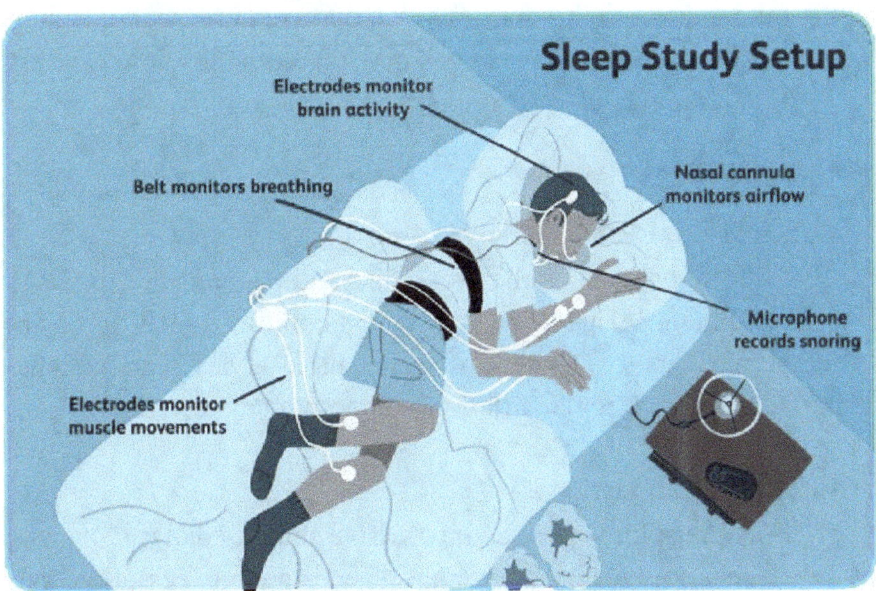

Patient Education Principles

1. Understanding Sleep Apnea
   - Patients should have a clear understanding of what sleep apnea is, including its causes, symptoms, and potential health impacts. Visual aids, such as diagrams and videos, can enhance comprehension.

2. Treatment Options and Their Importance
   - Explaining the various treatment options, including CPAP, lifestyle modifications, and surgical interventions, helps patients make informed decisions. Emphasize the benefits of treatment for overall health and quality of life.
3. Addressing Misconceptions
   - Address common misconceptions about sleep apnea and its treatments. For example, some patients may believe that CPAP is uncomfortable or that surgery is the only solution. Providing accurate information can alleviate concerns.
4. Setting Realistic Expectations
   - Help patients set realistic expectations for treatment outcomes. For instance, CPAP may require an adjustment period, and lifestyle changes may take time to show benefits. Encouraging patience and persistence is key.

Self-Management Strategies

1. Adherence to CPAP Therapy
   - Educate patients on the proper use and maintenance of CPAP equipment. Tips for improving comfort, such as using humidifiers or trying different mask styles, can enhance adherence. Regular follow-up appointments can address any issues.
2. Lifestyle Modifications
   - Encourage patients to adopt lifestyle changes that can improve sleep apnea, such as weight loss, smoking cessation, and reducing alcohol consumption. Provide resources, such as diet plans and exercise programs, to support these changes.
3. Positional Therapy
   - For patients with positional OSA, teach strategies to avoid sleeping on their backs, such as using positional pillows or wearable devices. Demonstrating these techniques can increase their effectiveness.

4. Sleep Hygiene Practices
   - Educate patients on good sleep hygiene practices, such as maintaining a regular sleep schedule, creating a comfortable sleep environment, and avoiding stimulants before bedtime. Simple changes can significantly improve sleep quality.
5. Monitoring Symptoms and Progress
   - Encourage patients to keep a sleep diary to track their symptoms, treatment adherence, and any changes in their condition. Regularly reviewing this diary with their healthcare provider can help monitor progress and make necessary adjustments.

Resources for Ongoing Support

1. Support Groups
   - Connecting patients with support groups, either in-person or online, can provide emotional support and practical advice from others who are managing sleep apnea. Peer support can enhance motivation and adherence.
2. Educational Materials
   - Provide patients with brochures, videos, and websites that offer reliable information about sleep apnea. Resources from reputable organizations, such as the American Academy of Sleep Medicine, can be particularly helpful.
3. Mobile Apps and Technology
   - Recommend mobile apps designed to support sleep apnea management. These apps can offer features such as symptom tracking, CPAP usage monitoring, and reminders for medication or appointments.
4. Regular Follow-Up
   - Schedule regular follow-up appointments to monitor treatment progress, address any concerns, and make necessary adjustments. Continuity of care is essential for effective long-term management.

Patient education and self-management are critical components of successful sleep apnea treatment. By equipping patients with knowledge and practical strategies, healthcare providers can empower them to take an active role in managing their condition. Ongoing support and resources further enhance patient engagement and improve outcomes.

DISCUSSION QUESTIONS

- How might emerging technologies, such as hypoglossal nerve stimulation or positional therapy devices, revolutionize the treatment of sleep apnea?
- What are the potential ethical and practical considerations in implementing advanced therapeutic approaches, and how can healthcare providers ensure equitable access to these treatments?

MODULE FIVE

LESSON ONE: SPECIAL CONSIDERATIONS IN PEDIATRIC SLEEP APNEA

Pediatric sleep apnea, while less common than in adults, presents unique challenges and considerations. Early diagnosis and intervention are crucial for preventing long-term health consequences in children. This lesson explores the causes, symptoms, diagnosis, and treatment of sleep apnea in pediatric patients, along with special considerations for managing the condition in this population.

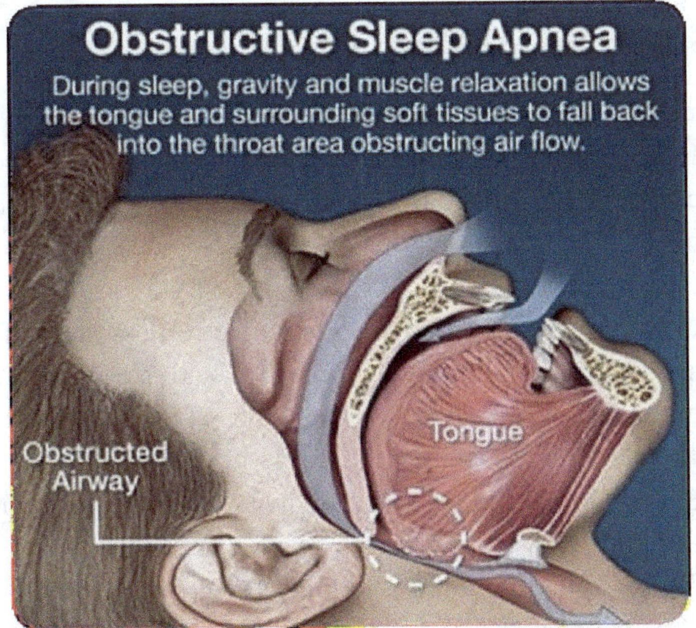

Causes of Pediatric Sleep Apnea

1. Adenotonsillar Hypertrophy
   - Enlarged tonsils and adenoids are the most common cause of obstructive sleep apnea (OSA) in children. This condition can obstruct the upper airway, particularly during sleep.

2. Obesity
   - Childhood obesity is a significant risk factor for OSA. Excess fat deposits around the neck and throat can narrow the airway and contribute to obstructive events.
3. Craniofacial Abnormalities
   - Structural abnormalities, such as a recessed chin or a narrow airway, can predispose children to OSA. Conditions like Down syndrome and Pierre Robin sequence are associated with higher risks.
4. Neuromuscular Disorders
   - Neuromuscular disorders that affect muscle tone and control can contribute to sleep apnea in children. Conditions such as cerebral palsy and muscular dystrophy are examples.

Symptoms of Pediatric Sleep Apnea

1. Snoring and Pauses in Breathing
   - Loud snoring, gasping, or choking sounds during sleep are common indicators of OSA in children. Parents may also observe pauses in breathing.
2. Restless Sleep
   - Children with sleep apnea often have restless sleep, frequent awakenings, and may assume unusual sleep positions to maintain airway patency.
3. Daytime Sleepiness and Behavioral Issues
   - Excessive daytime sleepiness, irritability, hyperactivity, and difficulty concentrating can result from poor sleep quality. These symptoms may be mistaken for attention deficit hyperactivity disorder (ADHD).
4. Growth and Developmental Concerns
   - Untreated sleep apnea can impact growth and development. Children may experience failure to thrive, poor weight gain, or developmental delays.

DIAGNOSIS OF PEDIATRIC SLEEP APNEA

1. Clinical Evaluation
   - A thorough clinical evaluation, including a detailed medical history and physical examination, is essential. Questions about snoring, sleep patterns, and daytime behavior can provide valuable clues.
2. **Polysomnography**
   - Overnight polysomnography (sleep study) is the gold standard for diagnosing sleep apnea in children. It measures various physiological parameters, including respiratory effort, oxygen saturation, and sleep stages.
3. Home Sleep Apnea Testing (HSAT)
   - While less common in children, HSAT may be considered in certain cases where polysomnography is not feasible. However, its use in pediatrics is limited and requires careful consideration.
4. Imaging Studies
   - Imaging studies, such as lateral neck X-rays or MRI, may be used to assess airway anatomy and identify structural abnormalities contributing to sleep apnea.

TREATMENT OF PEDIATRIC SLEEP APNEA

1. Adenotonsillectomy
   - Surgical removal of the tonsils and adenoids (adenotonsillectomy) is the first-line treatment for OSA caused by adenotonsillar hypertrophy. This procedure can significantly improve airway patency and alleviate symptoms.
2. Positive Airway Pressure Therapy
   - Continuous positive airway pressure (CPAP) or bilevel positive airway pressure (BiPAP) therapy may be used in children who do not respond to or are not candidates for surgery. These devices help keep the airway open during sleep.

3. Weight Management
   - For children with obesity-related OSA, weight management through diet, exercise, and behavioral interventions is crucial. Addressing obesity can reduce the severity of sleep apnea and improve overall health.
4. Orthodontic Interventions
   - Orthodontic treatments, such as rapid maxillary expansion (RME), can help widen the upper airway in children with craniofacial abnormalities. These interventions are often combined with other treatments.
5. **Medication**
   - In some cases, medications such as intranasal corticosteroids or leukotriene receptor antagonists may be used to reduce airway inflammation and improve symptoms.

SPECIAL CONSIDERATIONS

1. Developmental and Behavioral Support
   - Children with sleep apnea may require additional support for developmental and behavioral issues. Collaboration with pediatric specialists, such as developmental pediatricians and child psychologists, can provide comprehensive care.
2. Family Education and Support
   - Educating families about the condition, treatment options, and the importance of adherence to therapy is crucial. Support groups and counseling can help families cope with the challenges of managing pediatric sleep apnea.
3. Long-Term Monitoring
   - Regular follow-up appointments are essential to monitor treatment progress and adjust interventions as needed. Long-term monitoring helps ensure that children achieve optimal outcomes and prevent complications.

Pediatric sleep apnea requires a multidisciplinary approach to diagnosis and management. Early intervention and comprehensive care can significantly improve the health and well-being of affected children. By understanding the unique aspects of pediatric sleep apnea, healthcare providers can provide targeted and effective treatment, ensuring better outcomes for young patients.

DISCUSSION QUESTIONS

- How can healthcare providers effectively address common misconceptions about CPAP therapy to improve patient adherence?
- What are the most significant challenges patients face in adopting lifestyle modifications for managing sleep apnea, and how can these challenges be overcome?

MODULE SIX

LESSON ONE: SLEEP APNEA IN SPECIAL POPULATIONS

Sleep apnea affects diverse populations, each with unique challenges and considerations. Understanding how sleep apnea manifests and is managed in these special populations is crucial for providing effective and individualized care. This lesson explores sleep apnea in pregnant women, the elderly, and individuals with cardiovascular diseases, discussing specific diagnostic and treatment approaches for each group.

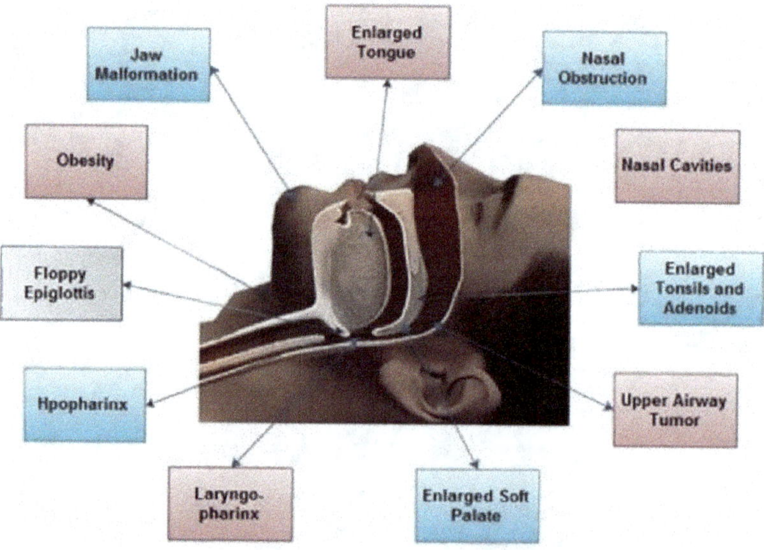

SLEEP APNEA IN PREGNANT WOMEN

1. Prevalence and Risk Factors
    - Pregnancy increases the risk of obstructive sleep apnea (OSA) due to physiological changes such as weight gain, fluid retention, and hormonal shifts. The prevalence of OSA in

pregnant women is estimated to be around 10-27%, with higher rates in obese and hypertensive women.

2. Impact on Maternal and Fetal Health
   - Untreated OSA during pregnancy is associated with adverse outcomes, including gestational hypertension, preeclampsia, gestational diabetes, preterm birth, and low birth weight. Identifying and managing OSA is vital for maternal and fetal health.

3. Diagnosis
   - Diagnosing OSA in pregnant women can be challenging due to overlapping symptoms with normal pregnancy changes, such as fatigue and frequent urination. Polysomnography remains the gold standard for diagnosis, but home sleep apnea testing (HSAT) may also be considered in certain cases.

4. Treatment
   - Continuous positive airway pressure (CPAP) therapy is the first-line treatment for OSA during pregnancy. It is effective in reducing symptoms and improving maternal and fetal outcomes. Lifestyle modifications, such as weight management and positional therapy, can also be beneficial.

5. Postpartum Considerations
   - Postpartum follow-up is essential to reassess and manage OSA. While some women may see improvement in their symptoms after delivery, others may continue to experience OSA and require ongoing treatment.

Sleep Apnea in the Elderly

1. Prevalence and Risk Factors
   - The prevalence of sleep apnea increases with age, affecting up to 20-30% of elderly individuals. Risk factors include age-related changes in airway anatomy, decreased muscle tone, and the presence of comorbid conditions such as obesity, hypertension, and heart disease.

2. Symptoms and Diagnosis
   - Symptoms of sleep apnea in the elderly can be nonspecific and overlap with other conditions, such as insomnia, cognitive impairment, and cardiovascular disease. Polysomnography remains the standard diagnostic tool, but careful clinical evaluation is necessary to differentiate sleep apnea from other sleep disorders.

3. Treatment
   - CPAP therapy is effective in treating sleep apnea in the elderly, improving sleep quality and reducing daytime sleepiness. Adherence to CPAP may be challenging due to cognitive and physical limitations, so education and support are crucial. Alternative treatments, such as mandibular advancement devices and positional therapy, may also be considered.

4. Comorbidities and Management
   - Managing sleep apnea in the elderly requires a comprehensive approach that addresses comorbid conditions such as hypertension, diabetes, and heart disease. Collaboration with geriatric specialists can help optimize treatment and improve overall health outcomes.

Sleep Apnea in Individuals with Cardiovascular Diseases

1. Prevalence and Impact
   - Sleep apnea is highly prevalent in individuals with cardiovascular diseases, including hypertension, heart failure, atrial fibrillation, and coronary artery disease. It is estimated that up to 50% of patients with heart failure have sleep apnea, predominantly central sleep apnea (CSA).

2. Pathophysiology
   - The interplay between sleep apnea and cardiovascular diseases involves complex mechanisms, including sympathetic nervous system activation, oxidative stress, inflammation, and endothelial dysfunction. These

mechanisms contribute to the development and progression of cardiovascular conditions.

3. Diagnosis
   - Screening for sleep apnea is essential in patients with cardiovascular diseases. Polysomnography is the preferred diagnostic tool, but HSAT may also be utilized. Cardiologists should be aware of the signs and symptoms of sleep apnea and refer patients for evaluation as needed.

4. Treatment
   - CPAP therapy is effective in treating OSA and can improve cardiovascular outcomes by reducing blood pressure, improving heart function, and decreasing arrhythmia incidence. Adaptive servo-ventilation (ASV) and bilevel positive airway pressure (BiPAP) are used to treat CSA. Lifestyle modifications, such as weight loss and smoking cessation, are also important.

5. Multidisciplinary Approach
   - Managing sleep apnea in individuals with cardiovascular diseases requires a multidisciplinary approach involving sleep specialists, cardiologists, and primary care providers. Coordinated care ensures comprehensive management and improved patient outcomes.

Sleep apnea presents unique challenges in special populations such as pregnant women, the elderly, and individuals with cardiovascular diseases. Tailoring diagnostic and treatment approaches to the specific needs of these groups is essential for effective management. By understanding the nuances of sleep apnea in these populations, healthcare providers can deliver individualized care that improves overall health and quality of life.

- How does the management of sleep apnea in children differ from that in adults, and what are the unique challenges healthcare providers face in pediatric cases?
- What role can parents and caregivers play in the successful treatment and management of sleep apnea in children, and what strategies can healthcare providers use to support them?

MODULE SEVEN

LESSON ONE: THE ROLE OF TELEMEDICINE IN SLEEP APNEA MANAGEMENT

Telemedicine has emerged as a powerful tool in healthcare, offering new opportunities for the diagnosis, treatment, and management of sleep apnea. The integration of telemedicine into sleep medicine can enhance patient access to care, improve treatment adherence, and streamline the management of this chronic condition. This lesson explores the role of telemedicine in sleep apnea management, including its benefits, challenges, and future directions.

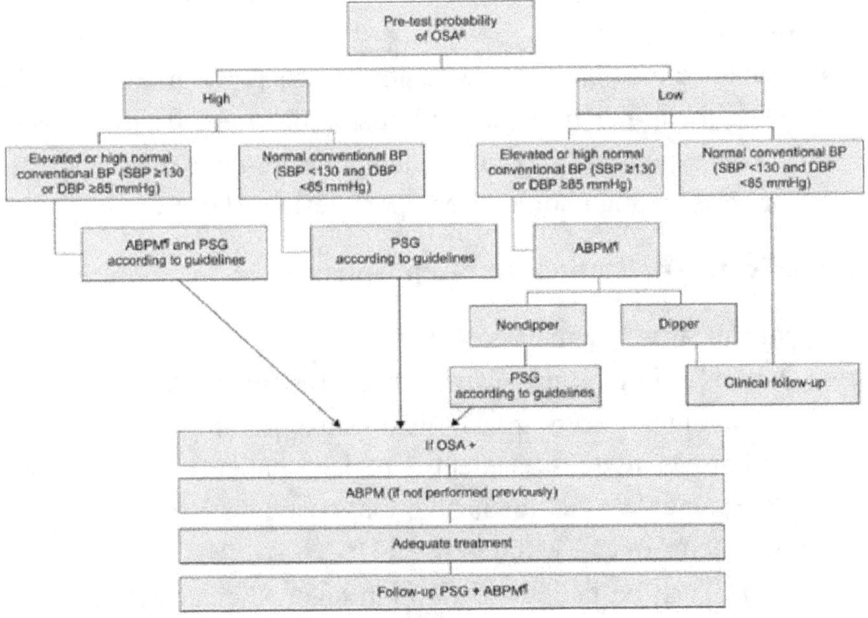

Benefits of Telemedicine in Sleep Apnea Management

1. Increased Access to Care
   - Telemedicine can overcome geographical barriers, allowing patients in remote or underserved areas to access specialized

sleep care. This is particularly important for individuals who have difficulty traveling to sleep centers due to mobility issues or lack of transportation.

2. Convenience and Flexibility
    - Telemedicine offers the convenience of virtual consultations, enabling patients to receive care from the comfort of their homes. This flexibility can enhance patient satisfaction and reduce the burden of in-person visits.

3. Improved Adherence to Treatment
    - Telemonitoring of CPAP adherence and efficacy can provide real-time data to healthcare providers, allowing for timely interventions and adjustments. Regular virtual follow-ups can help address patient concerns, troubleshoot issues, and reinforce the importance of treatment adherence.

4. Cost-Effectiveness
    - Telemedicine can reduce healthcare costs by minimizing the need for in-person visits and hospitalizations. It also reduces travel expenses for patients and can streamline the diagnostic process through home sleep apnea testing (HSAT).

Telemedicine Applications in Sleep Apnea

1. Initial Consultation and Screening
    - Virtual consultations can be used for initial evaluation and screening of sleep apnea. Healthcare providers can conduct comprehensive assessments, review patient histories, and determine the need for further diagnostic testing.

2. Home Sleep Apnea Testing (HSAT)
    - HSAT can be facilitated through telemedicine, with patients receiving devices by mail and receiving instructions via virtual platforms. This approach simplifies the diagnostic process and enhances patient convenience.

3. Treatment Initiation and Follow-Up
    - Telemedicine can be used to initiate CPAP therapy, with remote setup and education provided by sleep technologists.

Regular follow-up appointments via telemedicine allow for ongoing monitoring and support.

4. CPAP Telemonitoring
   - Remote monitoring of CPAP usage and effectiveness provides valuable data for healthcare providers. Patients can receive feedback and guidance on optimizing their therapy, improving adherence and outcomes.

5. Behavioral and Lifestyle Interventions
   - Telemedicine platforms can deliver behavioral interventions, such as cognitive-behavioral therapy for insomnia (CBT-I) and weight management programs. Virtual support groups and educational sessions can also be provided.

Challenges and Limitations

1. Technology Barriers
   - Limited access to technology and internet connectivity can be a barrier for some patients, particularly in rural or low-income areas. Addressing these disparities is crucial for equitable access to telemedicine.

2. Patient and Provider Acceptance
   - Acceptance and comfort with telemedicine vary among patients and providers. Education and training can help increase familiarity and confidence in using telemedicine platforms.

3. Data Security and Privacy
   - Ensuring the security and privacy of patient data is a significant concern in telemedicine. Compliance with regulations such as the Health Insurance Portability and Accountability Act (HIPAA) is essential to protect patient information.

4. Reimbursement and Policy Issues
   - Reimbursement policies for telemedicine services can vary, impacting the financial viability for providers and

accessibility for patients. Advocacy for consistent and fair reimbursement policies is needed.

Future Directions

1. Integration with Wearable Technology
   - Combining telemedicine with wearable devices that monitor sleep patterns, respiratory events, and oxygen levels can enhance the diagnosis and management of sleep apnea. These devices can provide continuous data and early detection of issues.
2. Artificial Intelligence (AI) and Machine Learning
   - AI and machine learning can analyze large volumes of sleep data to identify patterns, predict treatment outcomes, and personalize care. These technologies have the potential to enhance the accuracy and efficiency of telemedicine in sleep apnea management.
3. Expansion of Telemedicine Services
   - Expanding telemedicine services to include comprehensive sleep wellness programs, multidisciplinary care teams, and integration with primary care can improve overall sleep health and patient outcomes.

Telemedicine offers significant benefits for the management of sleep apnea, including increased access to care, convenience, improved treatment adherence, and cost-effectiveness. While challenges remain, the continued integration of telemedicine into sleep medicine, supported by technological advancements and policy changes, holds promise for enhancing patient care and outcomes

DISCUSSION QUESTIONS

- What are the key differences in diagnosing and treating sleep apnea in pregnant women compared to the general population, and how can healthcare providers address these differences?

- How does sleep apnea in the elderly impact their overall health, and what specific considerations should be taken into account when managing their condition?

49

CONCLUSION

Sleep apnea is a pervasive and potentially severe condition that significantly impacts patient health and quality of life. As healthcare providers, it is imperative to possess a thorough understanding of the complexities associated with diagnosing, treating, and managing sleep apnea. This comprehensive course has provided an in-depth exploration of the various aspects of sleep apnea, from its pathophysiology and clinical manifestations to the latest advancements in diagnostic techniques and treatment options.

Participants have gained valuable insights into the physiological mechanisms underlying sleep apnea, the importance of recognizing clinical signs and symptoms, and the use of diagnostic tools such as polysomnography and home sleep apnea testing. The course has emphasized the necessity of creating individualized treatment plans that include CPAP therapy, oral appliances, surgical interventions, and medication management, as well as the crucial role of lifestyle modifications and behavioral therapy in achieving long-term patient adherence and improved outcomes. As

REFERENCES

- Berry, R. B., Budhiraja, R., Gottlieb, D. J., Gozal, D., Iber, C., Kapur, V. K., Marcus, C. L., Mehra, R., Parthasarathy, S., Quan, S. F., Redline, S., Strohl, K. P., Davidson Ward, S. L., & Tangredi, M. M. (2012). *Rules for scoring respiratory events in sleep: update of the 2007 AASM Manual for the Scoring of Sleep and Associated Events. Journal of Clinical Sleep Medicine*, 8(5)

- Caples, S. M., Gami, A. S., & Somers, V. K. (2005). *Obstructive sleep apnea. Annals of Internal Medicine*, 142(3)

- Chervin, R. D., & Aldrich, M. S. (1999). *The Epworth Sleepiness Scale may not reflect objective measures of sleepiness or sleep apnea. Neurology*, 52(1).

- Epstein, L. J., Kristo, D., Strollo, P. J., Friedman, N., Malhotra, A., Patil, S. P., Ramar, K., Rogers, R., Schwab, R. J., Weaver, E. M., & Weinstein, M. D. (2009). *Clinical guideline for the evaluation, management and long-term care of obstructive sleep apnea in adults. Journal of Clinical Sleep Medicine*, 5(3).

- Guilleminault, C., Tilkian, A., & Dement, W. C. (1976). *The sleep apnea syndromes. Annual Review of Medicine*, 27(1)

- Iber, C., Ancoli-Israel, S., Chesson, A. L., & Quan, S. F. (2007). *The AASM manual for the scoring of sleep and associated events: rules, terminology and technical specifications. American Academy of Sleep Medicine.*

- Kushida, C. A., Littner, M. R., Morgenthaler, T., Alessi, C. A., Bailey, D., Coleman, J., Friedman, L., Hirshkowitz, M., Kapen, S., Kramer, M., Lee-Chiong, T., Owens, J., Pancer, J., & Wise, M. (2006). *Practice parameters for the treatment of snoring and obstructive sleep apnea with oral appliances: an update for 2005.*